....

From

....

Date

....

© 2011 by Barbour Publishing, Inc.

Written and compiled by Todd Hafer.

Daily readings without an attribution are written by Todd Hafer.

ISBN 978-1-61626-403-1

All rights reserved. No part of this publication may be reproduced or transmitted for commercial purposes, except for brief quotations in printed reviews, without written permission of the publisher.

All scripture quotations, unless otherwise noted, are taken from the HOLY BIBLE, NEW INTERNATIONAL VERSION®. NIV®. Copyright © 1973, 1978, 1984, 2011 by Biblica, Inc.™ Used by permission. All rights reserved worldwide.

Scripture quotations marked KJV are taken from the King James Version of the Bible.

Scripture quotations marked MSG are from THE MESSAGE. Copyright © by Eugene H. Peterson 1993, 1994, 1995, 1996, 2000, 2001, 2002. Used by permission of NavPress Publishing Group.

Scripture quotations marked NLT are taken from the *Holy Bible*. New Living Translation copyright © 1996, 2004, 2007 by Tyndale House Foundation. Used by permission of Tyndale House Publishers, Inc. Carol Stream, Illinois 60188. All rights reserved.

Scripture quotations marked NRSV are taken from the New Revised Standard Version Bible, copyright 1989, Division of Christian Education of the National Council of the Churches of Christ in the United States of America. Used by permission. All rights reserved.

Scripture quotations marked CEV are from the Contemporary English Version, copyright © 1991, 1992, 1995 by American Bible Society. Used by permission.

Scripture quotations marked NKJV are taken from the New King James Version®. Copyright © 1982 by Thomas Nelson, Inc. Used by permission. All rights reserved.

Scripture quotations marked NIrV are taken from the Holy Bible, NEW INTERNATIONAL READER'S VERSION®. Copyright © 1996, 1998 Biblica. All rights reserved throughout the world. Used by permission of Biblica.

Scripture quotations marked NCV are taken from the New Century Version of the Bible, copyright © 2005 by Thomas Nelson, Inc. Used by permission.

Scripture quotations marked NASB are taken from the New American Standard Bible, © 1960, 1962, 1963, 1968, 1971, 1972, 1973, 1975, 1977, 1995 by The Lockman Foundation. Used by permission.

Scripture quotations marked AMP are taken from the Amplified® Bible, © 1954, 1958, 1962, 1964, 1965, 1987 by The Lockman Foundation. Used by permission.

Scripture quotations marked TNIV are taken from the Holy Bible, Today's New International® Version, TNIV©. Copyright 2001, 2005 by International Bible Society®. Used by permission of International Bible Society®. All rights reserved worldwide. "TNIV" and "Today's New International Version" are trademarks registered in the United States Patent and Trademark Office by International Bible Society®.

Published by Barbour Publishing, Inc., P.O. Box 719, Uhrichsville, Ohio 44683, www.barbourbooks.com

Our mission is to publish and distribute inspirational products offering exceptional value and biblical encouragement to the masses.

Printed in China.

365 Little Reasons to Celebrate Today!

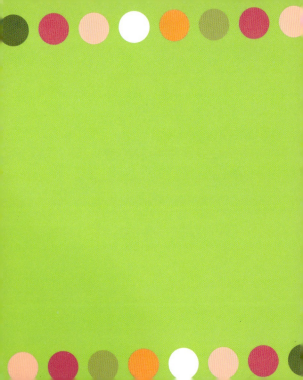

DAY 1

The Lord of Your Day

The Lord stands above the new day, for God has made it. All restlessness, all impurity, all worry and anxiety flee before Him.

DIETRICH BONHOEFFER

Day 2

Your Personal God

God, your loving Creator, wants you to experience Him firsthand. So read His book. Listen to His music. Hear His modern-day prophets (pastors, youth pastors, singers, authors, and musicians). Take time to be still in God's presence. Ask Him to fill you with His love.

Day 3

Today's Thought

Today, right now,
is a gift; that's why
it's called the *present*.

Day 4

Soul Food

Physical food is great, but the spiritual food God feeds us keeps us full— full of joy, full of hope, and full of love. His food is, truly, *soul food*.

Dream Big

Whatever you can
do or dream you can,
begin it. Boldness has beauty,
power, and magic in it.

JOHANN WOLFGANG VON GOETHE

Day 6

The Secret of Happiness

Happiness is only in loving.

Leo Tolstoy

Day 7

God Is Faithful

God assured us, "I'll never let you down, never walk off and leave you."

HEBREWS 13:5 MSG

Day 8

Today's Thought

Our Father God offers
us a cup of forgiveness
that is bottomless.

Day 9

To Ask Is to Receive

God has promised us that if we ask for His wisdom, He will share it. And how often does that sharing come to us through the insights and life experiences of our brothers and sisters in the faith!

DAY 10

Today's Top Five Reasons to Smile

1. Sunsets.
2. Dark chocolate is good for you!
3. Free samples at the grocery store.
4. Even water comes in flavors these days.
5. The memory of your first kiss.

Day 11

Happiness Overkill?

Unbroken happiness is a bore:
it should have ups and downs.

MOLIÉRE

Day 12

The Perfect Giver

God has gifted each
of us with abilities.
And He never makes a mistake.
His gifts are never the wrong
size or style—or inappropriate
in any way. No one has
ever needed to return
a gift from God.

Day 13

Today's Thought

If you reach out in love
to a difficult person in your life,
you can reduce your list
of enemies by one and gain
a friend at the same time.

DAY 14

For Your Inspiration...

Need a boost of inspiration? Consider real estate magnate Zell Kravinsky. He's given almost all of his $45 million fortune to health-related charities. But there's more. After learning that thousands of people die annually while waiting for kidney transplants, Kravinsky contacted a local hospital and donated one of his kidneys—to a stranger.

Day 15

On Moses and stress...

Stressed out?
Don't give up; Moses
was once a basket case.

DAY 16

Sharing the Light

Sometimes our light goes out but is nurtured into flame by another human being. Each of us owes deepest thanks to those who have rekindled this light.

ALBERT SCHWEITZER

Day 17

A Modern Beatitude

Blessed are you when
you have little stumbles,
for they prevent big falls.

DAY 18

The Love Decision

The Lord of all creation,
who knew you before you were born,
has decided to love you. Despite your
mistakes. Despite the indifference you
might feel toward Him sometimes.
Jesus loves you. He is committed
to you. He will faithfully forgive,
unconditionally accept,
and perfectly love you always.
He makes that effort every day.

Day 19

Seek and You Shall Find

Those who search will surely find me.

PROVERBS 8:17 NLT

Day 20

The Magic of Naps

No day is so bad that it can't be fixed with a nap.

CARRIE SNOW

Day 21

A Blessing for You

May the road
rise up to meet you.
May the wind be
always at your back.
May the sun shine
warm on your face;
the rains fall soft
upon your fields,
and until we meet again,
may God hold you
in the palm of His hand.

Traditional Gaelic Blessing

Day 22

The Power of Kindness

This world can be unkind sometimes, so when you're willing to show a little kindness and treat people the way Jesus would treat them, amazing things can happen. One random act of kindness can rock someone's world.

Day 23

The Good Shepherd

*The LORD is my shepherd,
I shall not want. He makes
me lie down in green pastures;
he leads me beside still waters;
he restores my soul. He leads
me in right paths for
his name's sake.*

Psalm 23:1–3 NRSV

DAY 24

Beginnings

Beginnings are wonderful things: they're free, they're full of possibilities, and everyone gets a new one every day. What will you do with yours today?

Day 25

No Fear Here

I am not afraid of tomorrow,
for I have seen yesterday,
and I love today.

William Allen White

DAY 26

Today's Top Five Reasons to Smile

1. Friday is never that far away.
2. Luggage on wheels.
3. High-definition TV.
4. The smell of freshly brewed coffee.
5. Free refills.

Day 27

On the Money

If you want to know
what God thinks of money,
just look at the people
He gave it to.

Dorothy Parker

Day 28

How High, How Far?

As high as heaven is over the earth, so strong is his love to those who fear him. And as far as sunrise is from sunset, he has separated us from our sins. As parents feel for their children, God feels for those who fear him.

PSALM 103:11–13 MSG

DAY 29

The Happy Way

Happiness is not
a state to arrive at,
but a manner of traveling.

MARGARET LEE RUNBECK

Day 30

Your Personal Stress Bearer

Cast all your anxiety on him because he cares for you.

1 Peter 5:7

Day 31

Surrounded by Inspiration

Insight and inspiration
are all around us—from a song
lyric heard on the radio,
to a random observation from
a child. After all, God works
in mysterious ways!

Day 32

Today's Thought

What if every sunrise is God's little way of saying, "Lighten up"?

Day 33

A Modern Beatitude

Blessed are the flexible,
for they shall never be
bent out of shape.

Day 34

Your Refuge

The LORD is good, a refuge in times of trouble. He cares for those who trust in him.

Nahum 1:7 TNIV

Day 35

The Ultimate Makeover

Love is the greatest
beautifier in the universe.

MAY CHRISTIE

Day 36

Today's Thought

It's good to know life has a lot to offer you, but even better to know that you have a lot to offer life!

Day 37

Success vs. Happiness

Success is getting what you want; happiness is wanting what you get.

CHARLES F. KETTERING

Day 38

Be strong

Be strong and courageous, and act; do not fear nor be dismayed, for the Lord God, my God, is with you. He will not fail you nor forsake you.

1 Chronicles 28:20 NASB

Day 39

The Power of Passion

One person with passion is better than forty who are merely interested.

TOM CONNELLAN

DAY 40

You Know It's Time to Join Your Church's Seniors Group When...

1. You try to straighten out the wrinkles in your socks—then realize you aren't wearing socks.

2. Even when you stay home, your back goes out.

3. Getting ready for church, it takes you twice as long to look half as good.

DAY 41

Pray Your Way to Greatness

When a believing person prays, great things happen.

JAMES 5:16 NCV

DAY 42

The Value of Failure

Success and failure are greatly overrated. But failure gives you a whole lot more to talk about.

HILDEGARD KNEF

Day 43

If You Believe...

Anything is possible if a person believes.

MARK 9:23 NLT

Day 44

Today's Thought

Noah was a brave man who set sail in a wooden boat that included at least two termites as passengers.

Day 45

Five Awesome Things God Says about You

1. You are God's hands and feet (Proverbs 3:27).
2. When you help others, you also help yourself (Proverbs 11:25).
3. You can embrace others with your words (Proverbs 24:26).
4. You were created to make a positive difference in the world (Ephesians 2:10).
5. You can help fight others' battles (2 Corinthians 1:10).

DAY 46

Imagine That!

Imagination is more important than knowledge.

ALBERT EINSTEIN

Day 47

Take the Plunge

Throw yourselves into the work of the Master, confident that nothing you do for him is a waste of time or effort.

1 CORINTHIANS 15:58 MSG

Day 48

Family Is Heavenly

A happy family is but
an earlier heaven.

AMERICAN PROVERB

Day 49

Today's Thought

Every day is a wonderful chance to be what you've dreamed. . .to do what you've imagined.

DAY 50

How to Be Blessed

Jesus said, "You're blessed when you're content with just who you are—no more, no less."

MATTHEW 5:5 MSG

Day 51

Today's Thought

What a caterpillar calls
the end of the world,
God calls a butterfly.

Day 52

Today's Top Five Reasons to Smile

1. Sunrises.
2. Bendy straws.
3. Most elevators don't play "elevator music" anymore.
4. Fresh-squeezed lemonade.
5. The National Do-Not-Call List.

DAY 53

Kindness Matters

No act of kindness,
no matter how small,
is ever wasted.

AESOP

Day 54

The Laughter Connection

Laughter is the shortest
distance between two people.

VICTOR BORGE

Day 55

Like a Rock

*You will keep in perfect peace
those whose minds are steadfast,
because they trust in you.
Trust in the Lord forever,
for the Lord, the Lord himself,
is the Rock eternal.*

Isaiah 26:3–4

Day 56

Future Tense

The best thing about the future is that it comes only one day at a time.

ABRAHAM LINCOLN

Day 57

Knicker Knots

Don't get your knickers in a knot. Nothing is solved, and it just makes you walk funny.

KATHRYN CARPENTER

Day 58

Today's Thought

Life is way more interesting if you *don't* have all the answers.

Day 59

You Never Know...

You never know when
one kind act, or one word
of encouragement,
can change a life forever.

ZIG ZIGLAR

Day 60

Hide & Seek?

God pursues those He loves
to the ends of the earth.
Will you let Him find you?

THELMA WELLS

Day 61

God's Plans for You

"For I know the plans I have for you," declares the Lord, "plans to prosper you and not to harm you, plans to give you hope and a future. Then you will call upon me and come and pray to me, and I will listen to you. You will seek me and find me when you seek me with all your heart."

Jeremiah 29:11–13

DAY 62

Today's Top Five Reasons to Smile

1. They didn't make a sequel to *Casablanca*.
2. Online bill pay.
3. Caller ID.
4. Your ever-growing collection of social-network friends.
5. LARGE-PRINT BOOKS.

Day 63

In Good Hands

I have held many things in my hands, and I have lost them all; but whatever I have placed in God's hands, that I still possess.

Martin Luther

Day 64

Today's Thought

Rest today in the knowledge that you cannot go anywhere—even the depths of despair—where God cannot reach.

Day 65

Waiting for You

The Lord of all creation
is waiting for you.
You might not know Him well,
but He knows you. He wants
to hear from you. So don't
wait another second.
Open your eyes; open your heart.
God wants to communicate
with you right now!

DAY 66

Thank Heaven for Families

Thank heaven for a family
that lifts me when I'm low,
loves me when I'm unlovable,
and makes me believe
that I am the man
they think I am.

TAYLOR MORGAN

Day 67

It's All Good

We know that God causes everything to work together for the good of those who love God and are called according to his purpose for them.

Romans 8:28 NLT

DAY 68

It's a Wonderful World

I still find each day too short
for all the thoughts I want to think,
all the walks I want to take,
all the books I want to read,
and all the friends I want to see.
The longer I live, the more my
mind dwells upon the beauty
and the wonder of the world.

JOHN BURROUGHS

DAY 69

Singing the Blues

I merely took the energy it takes to pout and wrote some blues.

DUKE ELLINGTON

DAY 70

Youth vs. Age

Youth is a gift of nature,
but age is a work of art.

GARSON KANIN

DAY 71

Lavished with Love

See what great love the Father has lavished on us, that we should be called children of God! And that is what we are!

1 John 3:1

Day 72

The Almighty and You

The same God who guides the stars in their courses, who directs the earth in its orbit, who feeds the burning furnace of the sun and keeps the stars perpetually burning with their fires—the same God has promised to supply thy strength.

Charles Spurgeon

Day 73

You Know It's Time to Join Your Church's Seniors Group When...

1. It takes you longer to rest up than it did to get tired.

2. The only birthday gift you want from your fellow parishioners is *not* to be reminded of your age.

3. At the breakfast table, you hear lots of *Snap! Crackle!* and *Pop!* But you aren't eating cereal.

DAY 74

The Power of One

One great, strong, unselfish soul in every community could actually redeem the world.

ELBERT HUBBARD

Day 75

Today's Thought

Technically, a slice of carrot cake counts as a serving of vegetables.

Day 76

Spreading Happiness

Happiness seems
made to be shared.

PIERRE CORNEILLE

Miracle Seeds

Out of difficulties
grow miracles.

JEAN DE LA BRUYÈRE

Day 78

Today's Thought

How blessed you are to have a Lord and Savior who cares enough to provide rules to help you achieve the abundant life Jesus has promised!

DAY 79

Food for thought

The journey of faith is long—
better take snacks!

DAN TAYLOR

DAY 80

Top Five Things We'll Get to Do in Heaven

(Besides Sitting on a Cloud and Playing the Harp)

1. Tune the harps.
2. Double-check the harp inventory.
3. Tweet regularly on Twitter.com/harpnut.
4. Oversee production of "Just Harpy to Be Here!" bumper stickers.
5. Complain about how prolonged cloud-sitting/harp-playing makes one's foot fall asleep.

Day 81

Be Still

Be still, and know that I am God.

PSALM 46:10 KJV

DAY 82

Can Do

Those who say it cannot
be done should not interrupt
the person doing it.

CHINESE PROVERB

Day 83

Q&A

It's a blessing to learn to appreciate life's questions. You can learn much about yourself—and life itself—from the questions that emerge daily. Know that God, Master Architect of the Universe, has chosen to reach past the sun, the moon, and the stars to take your hand and lead you.

DAY 84

Today's Thought

Even if you have neglected your relationship with God, He still yearns to be close to you. He holds no grudges; instead, He holds His people close to His heart.

Day 85

On Nobodies and Somebodies...

I'll call nobodies and make them somebodies; I'll call the unloved and make them beloved. In the place where they yelled out, "You're nobody!" they're calling you "God's living children."

ROMANS 9:25–26 MSG

DAY 86

Today's Top Five Reasons to Smile

1. Milk Duds are low fat.
2. Room service.
3. Your every smile exercises twenty-six muscles!
4. Low-fat ice cream.
5. Self-cleaning ovens.

Day 87

Success

To laugh often and much;
To win the respect of
intelligent people and
the affection of children;
To appreciate beauty,
to find the best in others;
To know even one life
has breathed easier
because you have lived.
This is to have succeeded.

Ralph Waldo Emerson

Day 88

Today's Thought

True happiness is knowing that you are constantly in the process of becoming what you were meant to be.

Day 89

True Immortality

*The world and its desires pass away,
but whoever does the will
of God lives forever.*

1 John 2:17

Day 90

Today's Thought

Did the biblical prophets get tired of friends constantly asking if the weekend weather would be nice for a picnic?

Day 91

A Quote for the Ages

Age is just a number.

STEVE CARLTON (AT AGE 64)

DAY 92

Your Compassion Guarantee

Because of the LORD's great love we are not consumed, for his compassions never fail. They are new every morning; great is your faithfulness.

LAMENTATIONS 3:22–23

DAY 93

Mission Impossible?

It's kind of fun to do the impossible.

WALT DISNEY

DAY 94

Today's Thought

The light of God's divine love is so brilliant that it makes everything else dull in comparison. God's light is the one we should run to, because only in that light can we find true happiness and fulfillment.

Day 95

Golden Rules

Abiding by God's commandments ensures our protection, fulfillment, peace, and well-being. Life's quality is a product of our choices, and we don't always have the information, wisdom, or perspective to make the best choices. That's why our wise and loving God has given us rules to live by.

DAY 96

Today's Thought

Gambling is regarded as a sin. However, church raffles and Bingo are okay. Can someone please explain?

Day 97

Make Me an Instrument

Lord, make me an
instrument of Thy peace;
where there is hatred,
let me sow love;
where there is injury, pardon;
where there is doubt, faith;
where there is despair, hope;
where there is darkness, light;
and where there is sadness, joy.

SAINT FRANCIS OF ASSISI

Day 98

Be Strong

*Be strong and courageous.
Do not be afraid;
do not be discouraged,
for the LORD your God will be
with you wherever you go.*

JOSHUA 1:9

Day 99

On Kindness...

Let no one ever come to you without leaving better and happier. Be the living expression of God's kindness: kindness in your face, kindness in your eyes, kindness in your smile.

Mother Teresa

DAY 100

Three Perplexing Spiritual Questions

1. Are Mondays really "days that the Lord hath made"? (And if so, why hath He?)

2. If a pastor questions his wife's judgment while he's in the forest, with no one around to hear him, is he still wrong?

3. Why are church people so kind, polite, and sweet spirited— until you try to sit in their pew?

DAY 101

A Higher Power

My faith in God doesn't get rid of my healthy fear of climbing extreme heights, but it does help me deal with it. It takes away a lot of the pressure, because you know that God's not going to condemn you if you don't win. So there's nothing to worry about. When I see others competing, I wonder how I could compete if I didn't have faith in God.

KATIE BROWN, DIFFICULTY CLIMBER

DAY 102

A Fishy Excuse

Saint Peter halted a man at the entrance to heaven. "I'm sorry," the saint said, "but I cannot admit you. You've told too many lies." "C'mon, Pete, give me a break," the man pleaded. "After all, you were once a fisherman yourself!"

Day 103

Doing It All

I can do all things through Christ who strengthens me.

PHILIPPIANS 4:13 NKJV

Day 104

The Soul Hungers

My soul has had
enough chicken soup.
It wants chocolate!

CHERIE RAYBURN

DAY 105

Today's Thought

Why do people call a circumstance "God's Timing" only when they *don't* get what they want?

Day 106

Unending Encouragement

May our Lord Jesus Christ himself and God our Father encourage you and strengthen you in every good thing you do and say. God loved us, and through his grace he gave us a good hope and encouragement that continues forever.

2 Thessalonians 2:16–17 NCV

DAY 107

Today's Top Five Reasons to Smile

1. Self-stick postage stamps.
2. Warm and fluffy clothes and towels, fresh from the dryer.
3. More soda flavors than ever before!
4. Fresh-squeezed orange juice.
5. Milk shakes.

Day 108

A Mighty Fortress

Truly my soul finds rest in God. . . . Truly he is my rock and my salvation; he is my fortress, I will never be shaken.

Psalm 62:1–2

Day 109

Happiness Is Contagious

Whoever is happy will
make others happy, too.

MARK TWAIN

DaY 110

Possible Excuses to Use if You Get Caught Sleeping in Church

1. "When I donated blood yesterday, they told me this might happen."

2. "Someone must have put decaf in the fellowship-area coffeepot this morning."

3. "I wasn't sleeping; I was just deeply meditating on the sermon."

Day 111

Quality vs. Quantity

And in the end, it's not the years in your life that count. It's the life in your years.

ABRAHAM LINCOLN

Day 112

Three Ways to Tell You're an "Old School" Christian

1. All the verses you've memorized are from the King James Bible.
2. Most of those verses involve "smiting."
3. You know the fifth verse of every hymn with five verses.

DAY 113

A Faithful Forgiver

If we confess our sins, He is faithful and just to forgive us our sins and to cleanse us from all unrighteousness.

1 JOHN 1:9 NKJV

DAY 114

Joy's Secret Ingredient

Gratitude is the
key to happiness.

C. S. Lewis

DAY 115

Yes, I Can!

All things are possible with God.

MARK 10:27 NASB

Day 116

Today's Thought

If you prove to be a talented church volunteer, you'll be "volunteered" for everything. However, if you're really, really talented, you'll be able to get out of it.

Day 117

Fun Things to Say at Church Potlucks

1. "Is there a kosher meal available?"
2. "Is there a vegan meal available?"
3. "What exactly are the rules about gluttony?"
4. "So, I guess drinking the Kool-Aid is okay now?"
5. "Is it all right for me to designate who I'd like to be heimliched by... just in case?"

Day 118

The Beauty of Forgiveness

Humanity is never so beautiful
as when praying for forgiveness
or else forgiving another.

JEAN PAUL RICHTER

Day 119

Seeking and Finding

*Seek his will in all you do,
and he will show you
which path to take.*

Proverbs 3:6 NLT

Day 120

A Midlife Reminder

Now that I have entered midlife, I have learned a new rule: never apply makeup during a hot flash, because it will slide right off your face.

Anita Renfroe

DAY 121

Not Accurate, but True All the Same

A group of Sunday school students were tested on their Bible memory verses. A six-year-old boy stood to recite John 3:16. "I know this one," he assured the teacher. "Whosoever believeth in Jesus shall have ever-laughing life!" The teacher gave the boy partial credit.

DAY 122

Today's Thought

You're invited to
a party in heaven!

(Please, *please* RSVP.)

Day 123

Three (More) Signs You're an "Old School" Christian

1. On your calendar, every Sunday night and every Wednesday night is booked. *Forever.*
2. You approve of facial hair only when it's for a passion play.
3. All of your children have names from the Bible.

DAY 124

Today's Thought

There are advantages to getting older. For example, you can't nurse a grudge that you can't remember.

DAY 125

You Know It's Time to Join Your Church's Seniors Group When...

1. You sit in a rocking chair, but you can't get it started.
2. Your idea of weight lifting is standing up after a long sermon.
3. Your pastor compliments you on your patience, but your secret is that you just don't care anymore.

Day 126

Cheer Up!

*So be truly glad.
There is wonderful joy
ahead, even though you
have to endure many
trials for a little while.*

1 Peter 1:6 NLT

DAY 127

Back to the Future

When you forgive, you in no way change the past—but you sure do change the future.

BERNARD MELTZER

DAY 128

Top Ten Least Popular Bible Names

1. Judas
2. Mephibosheth
3. Bathsheba
4. Jezebel
5. Jehoshaphat
6. Methuselah
7. Kevin
8. Pontius
9. Sapphira
10. Ananias

DAY 129

Church Potluck Tip

Avoid any meat dish that bears tread marks.

Day 130

God Is Love, and So Is Dog

In a Sunday school class, students were asked to write a short prayer. One six-year-old fidgeted in his chair and nibbled his pencil for several minutes before committing his prayer to paper. It read, "Dear God, please help me be the person my dog thinks I am."

Day 131

The Best-Laid Plans

*The plans of the Lord
stand firm forever,
the purposes of his heart
through all generations.*

Psalm 33:11

Day 132

Can't Keep a Good Person Down

Though the righteous fall seven times, they rise again.

Proverbs 24:16

Day 133

The Perfect Prayer Partner

A great prayer partner keeps your secrets, laughs at your jokes, and has the wisdom, always, to know the difference.

Rev. Robert St. John

DAY 134

Today's Thought

Simon Peter and Andrew were fishermen. What did they do for vacation— take a week off to go accounting?

Day 135

Stumbling Toward Success

If we will only attempt to walk toward Him, He is pleased even with our stumbles.

C. S. Lewis

Day 136

The Treasure of a Friend

Treasure your friends,
every day. Don't pass up
an opportunity to tell them,
or show them, that you appreciate
how much they mean to your life.
Be there for them when they
need you, the way you hope
they'll be there for you.

Day 137

Trying Too Hard?

If only we'd stop *trying* to be happy, we'd have a pretty good time.

EDITH WHARTON

Day 138

Today's Thought

If 10 percent of my income is good enough for God, why isn't it good enough for the IRS?

Day 139

What the World Needs Now

What the world really
needs is more love
and less paperwork.

Pearl Bailey

DAY 140

One Matters

One person with courage makes a majority.

ANDREW JACKSON

DAY 141

Today's Thought

God will stop loving you—stop loving all of us—the same time water stops being wet.

DAY 142

Simpler Is Better

A hot dog at the ball game beats roast beef at the Ritz.

HUMPHREY BOGART

Day 143

Today's Thought

Jesus sees the real you and loves you so much that it boggles the mind. You can trust Him completely. He'll stand by your side no matter what. You can share with Him your secret fears, your hidden guilt. He is the most faithful friend you'll ever have. You're significant and valuable because His love makes you that way.

Day 144

Over and Under

What's over your head
is under God's feet.

Rev. Robert St. John

DAY 145

On Housework...

You make the beds,
you do the dishes,
and six months later
you have to start
all over again.

JOAN RIVERS

Day 146

Help for the Hurting

*For the Lord comforts
his people and will
have compassion
on his afflicted ones.*

Isaiah 49:13

Day 147

Did You Know?

1. You are a superstar (Philippians 2:15–16).
2. You are rich (1 Timothy 6:6).
3. God has great plans for you (Jeremiah 29:11).
4. God remembers every one of your tears (Psalm 56:8).
5. You make God sing (Zephaniah 3:17).

Day 148

A Matter of Choice

It's so important to know that you can choose to feel good. Most people don't think they have that choice.

NEIL SIMON

DAY 149

Your Fail-Safe

Cast your cares on the LORD and he will sustain you; he will never let the righteous be shaken.

PSALM 55:22

DAY 150

Today's Thought

Life is fragile—
handle with prayer.

DAY 151

Rest Assured

Rest today in the understanding that God's plan is good and His promises are true. He will make good on His promise to work all things for our good if we love and serve Him. We know with absolute certainty that He will be our comforter and our deliverer in our times of utmost pain and grief.

Day 152

A Sweet Joy

Friendship is one of
the sweetest joys of life.
Many might have failed beneath
the bitterness of their trial,
had they not found a friend.

CHARLES SPURGEON

DAY 153

Today's Thought

Can God inspire a sermon so boring that even God cannot stay awake through it?

Day 154

Blessed Are the Patient

God blesses those who patiently endure testing and temptation.

JAMES 1:12 NLT

DAY 155

A Prayer for This Day

I thank You, God,
for this most amazing day,
for the leaping greenly spirits of trees,
and for the blue dream of sky,
and for everything which is natural,
which is infinite, which is yes.

E. E. CUMMINGS

Day 156

Love Reciprocates

I have found that
if you love life,
life will love you back.

Arthur Rubenstein

Day 157

Rest for the Weary

*Come to me, all you
who are weary and burdened,
and I will give you rest.*

Matthew 11:28

DAY 158

Today's Thought

Consider this truth for a minute: Jesus is your friend. You may think of Jesus as your creator, your leader, your teacher, even the almighty Lord of your life. And He is all of those things. But Jesus is also your friend. "I've named you friends," He says (JOHN 15:15 MSG).

Day 159

The Creator and His Created

Putting your God-given talents to work is one of the most satisfying things you will ever do. As you do what God created you for, you gain a deep sense of purpose and become closer and more grateful to the One who gave you your talents. Few things are as beautiful as Creator and creation working together.

DAY 160

A Different Drummer

If a man does not keep pace with his companions, perhaps it is because he hears a different drummer. Let him step to the music which he hears, however measured or far away.

HENRY DAVID THOREAU

DAY 161

God's Sense of Humor

Gray hair is God's graffiti.

BILL COSBY

DAY 162

Ten Keys to Success

1. Believe when others doubt.
2. Learn while others loaf.
3. Decide while others delay.
4. Begin while others procrastinate.
5. Work while others wish.
6. Save while others spend.
7. Listen while others talk.
8. Smile while others scowl.
9. Compliment while others criticize.
10. Persist when others quit.

Day 163

Your Lifesaver

No water's too deep
with God as your floaties.

AMY TROWBRIDGE-YATES

Day 164

The Power and Beauty of Love

Love never gives up. Love cares more for others than for self. Love doesn't want what it doesn't have... doesn't force itself on others, isn't always "me first," doesn't fly off the handle, doesn't keep score of the sins of others...puts up with anything, trusts God always, always looks for the best, never looks back, but keeps going to the end.

1 Corinthians 13:4–7 MSG

Day 165

Ten Things to MAKE Besides Money

1. Time
2. Merry
3. Do
4. Up
5. Sense
6. Peace
7. Room
8. Waves
9. Amends
10. Believe

Day 166

The Nearest and Best

The best things are nearest:
breath in the nostrils, light in your eyes,
flowers at your feet, duties at your hand,
the path of God just before you.

ROBERT LOUIS STEVENSON

DAY 167

On Improving With Age...

The older I get,
the better I used to be.

LEE TREVINO

Day 168

When You're at the End of Your Rope...

You're blessed when you're at the end of your rope. With less of you there is more of God and his rule. You're blessed when you feel you've lost what is most dear to you. Only then can you be embraced by the One most dear to you.

Matthew 5:3–4 msg

DAY 169

It's Not Too Late...

It's never too late to be what you might have been.

GEORGE ELIOT

Day 170

Today's Thought

Jesus will listen to your thoughts, opinions, and concerns. No topic is off-limits. Nothing is too big or too small. You can approach Jesus just to tell Him how you feel, just to unburden all the thoughts and worries bouncing around in your head like sneakers in the dryer.

DAY 171

The Happiness Equation

A happy life is simply
the sum of many small,
happy moments.

PENNY KRUGMAN

Day 172

Where Is Success?

Success often lies just
the other side of failure.

Leo Buscaglia

Day 173

Unfathomable Love

We are so preciously loved by God
that we cannot even comprehend it.
No created being can ever know
how much and how sweetly and
tenderly God loves them.

Saint Julian of Norwich

Day 174

Safe and Secure

*The lines of purpose in your lives
never grow slack, tightly tied
as they are to your future in heaven,
kept taut by hope.*

Colossians 1:5 msg

DAY 175

Today's Thought

Jesus, in His broken body, absorbed every wrong thing you've ever done and ever will do. The sin is no longer yours. He made it His. The Bible says that Jesus "became sin." Then He died, taking all that sin down with Him. He was buried, but He out muscled death and rose to life. The sin stayed buried. You are free from it.

Day 176

Against the Wind

A certain amount of opposition is a great help to a person. Kites rise against the wind, not with it.

JOHN NEAL

Day 177

Ignorance Is Bliss?

You don't have to know everything to be happy—in fact, it helps.

RUSS EDIGER

Day 178

When a Little Means a Lot

Too often we underestimate
the power of a touch, a smile,
a kind word, a listening ear,
an honest compliment,
or the smallest act of caring,
all of which have the potential
to turn a life around.

Leo Buscaglia

Day 179

You're Closer Than You Think

Success is often just an idea away.

FRANK TYGER

Day 180

No Victim of Circumstance

The circumstances of our lives have as much power as we choose to give them.

David McNally

Day 181

In Christ

It's in Christ that we find out who we are and what we are living for.

Ephesians 1:11 MSG

Day 182

Life in Balance

Be aware of wonder.
Live a balanced life—
learn some and think some
and draw and paint and
sing and dance and play
and work every day some.

Robert Fulghum

Day 183

Today's Thought

You have a unique place in the world—a place only you can fill. Without you, history would be incomplete, like a jigsaw puzzle missing a vital piece. You are a one-of-a-kind, irreplaceable, incomparable treasure.

DaY 184

Trust Worthy

*I trust in you, O Lord;
I say, "You are my God."
My times are in your hand.*

PSALM 31:14–15 NRSV

DAY 185

Unstoppable!

Obstacles cannot crush me.
Every obstacle yields to stern resolve.
He who is fixed to a star does
not change his mind.

LEONARDO DA VINCI

DAY 186

Good Morning!

When we wake up
in the morning and turn
our soul toward You,
You are there first.

SOREN KIERKEGAARD

Day 187

Safe and Sound

You are my hiding place; you will protect me from trouble and surround me with songs of deliverance.

Psalm 32:7

DAY 188

Beauty in Diversity

Beauty comes in all ages, colors, shapes, and forms. God never makes junk.

KATHY IRELAND

DAY 189

Today's Thought

Remember always that the secret of success is how happily you climb—not how high.

DAY 190

Unending Happiness

The happiness that comes from doing good is a happiness that will never end.

CHINESE PROVERB

Day 191

How to Be Rich

I make myself rich by making my wants few.

HENRY DAVID THOREAU

Day 192

Fly Like an Eagle

Those who hope in the Lord will renew their strength. They will soar on wings like eagles; they will run and not grow weary, they will walk and not be faint.

Isaiah 40:31

Day 193

He Who Holds the Future

Every experience God gives us, every person He puts in our lives, is the perfect preparation for the future that only He can see.

CORRIE TEN BOOM

DAY 194

Today's Thought

Hang in there! Retirement is only _____ years away!

Day 195

God's Gift of Nature

Nature never did betray
the heart that loved her.

WILLIAM WORDSWORTH

DAY 196

Signs You're Working Too Hard

1. You try to enter your computer password on the microwave oven.
2. You have not played Solitaire with real cards in years.
3. When calling from home, you instinctively dial 9 to get an outside line.

DAY 197

Well Made

God made you as you are in order to use you as He planned.

J. C. MACAULEY

Day 198

Voice Recognition

*My sheep listen to my voice;
I know them, and they follow me.
I give them eternal life, and they
will never perish. No one can
snatch them away from me.*

JOHN 10:27–28 NLT

Day 199

Some Advice from Yogi

Stay alert—you can observe a lot by watching.

YOGI BERRA

DAY 200

Today's Thought

You are never alone.
There's Someone pulling for you.
Someone who knows you inside and
out. Someone who understands your
place in the big picture and knows
exactly where the puzzle piece that is
"you" belongs. He wants to help you
see yourself through His eyes.
He wants you to know you're
so much more than "enough."

Day 201

Road Map to Happiness?

Happiness cannot be traveled to, owned, earned, worn, or consumed. Happiness is the spiritual experience of living every minute with love, grace, and gratitude.

Denis Waitley

DAY 202

Your Heavenly Inheritance

*Praise be to the God and
Father of our Lord Jesus Christ!
In his great mercy he has given us
new birth into a living hope through
the resurrection of Jesus Christ from
the dead, and into an inheritance
that can never perish, spoil or fade.
This inheritance is kept in heaven for you.*

1 Peter 1:3–4

DAY 203

On Gossip...

Remember, if people
talk behind your back,
it only means you are
two steps ahead.

FANNIE FLAGG

Day 204

A Prayer for You

May your life become one of glad and unending praise to the Lord as you journey through this world and in the world that is to come!

Teresa of Avila

DAY 205

Blessings Abounding

*The faithful will
abound with blessings.*

PROVERBS 28:20 NRSV

DAY 206

Thoreau on Perspective

I would rather sit on a pumpkin and have it all to myself than be crowded on a velvet cushion.

HENRY DAVID THOREAU

Day 207

The Right Stuff

The name of the righteous is used in blessings.

PROVERBS 10:7

DAY 208

Excellence Vs. Perfection

I am careful not to confuse excellence with perfection. Excellence, I can reach for; perfection is God's business.

MICHAEL J. FOX

Day 209

God's Eyes and Ears

*The eyes of the Lord
watch over those who do right,
and his ears are open
to their prayers.*

1 Peter 3:12 NLT

DAY 210

No Small Thing

Is it so small a thing to
have enjoyed the sun,
to have lived light in the
spring, to have loved,
to have thought,
to have done?

MATTHEW ARNOLD

DAY 211

Jesus Is With You

For where two or three gather in my name, there am I with them.

MATTHEW 18:20

Day 212

You're a Living Poem

You are a living poem.
Some people are sonnets.
Some are limericks.
Some are haiku. But each
person is a unique work of art.
As a living poem, you are being
written one day at a time,
as both you and God
hold the pen.

VICKI KUYPER

Day 213

A Prayer from Saint Patrick

Christ with me,
Christ before me,
Christ behind me,
Christ in me,
Christ beneath me,
Christ above me,
Christ on my right,
Christ on my left,
Christ when I lie down,
Christ when I sit down,
Christ when I arise....

SAINT PATRICK

DAY 214

How Far Will You Go?

How far you go in life depends on your being tender with the young, compassionate with the aged, sympathetic with the striving, and tolerant of the weak and the strong. Because someday in life, you will have been all of these.

GEORGE WASHINGTON CARVER

DAY 215

One Lovely Action

All the beautiful sentiments
in the world weigh less than
a single lovely action.

JAMES RUSSELL LOWELL

Day 216

Today's Thought

"God is love." God does not just give love, He *is* love. That's His true identity. And God is never in danger of identity theft.

Day 217

Your Light Will Shine

If you spend yourselves in behalf of the hungry and satisfy the needs of the oppressed, then your light will rise in the darkness, and your night will become like the noonday.

Isaiah 58:10

DAY 218

Today's Thought

You can always be young at heart—even if you feel old everyplace else.

Day 219

Top Five Church Pickup Lines

1. "Hey, baby, what's your spiritual gift?"

2. "No, this pew isn't saved, but I sure am!"

3. "This sermon's dull—wanna try to start 'The Wave'?"

4. "Do you know I can bench-press an entire set of Bible commentaries?"

5. "Do you have a brother named Gabriel—because I'm sure you're an angel!"

Day 220

Today's Thought

Christ's love will carry you through whatever happens today, even if right now it feels impossible to make it to tomorrow.

Day 221

The Key to Failure

I don't know the key to success, but the key to failure is trying to please everybody.

BILL COSBY

Day 222

The Christian and the Lion

In ancient Rome, a lion chased a Christian. Eventually, the man realized the lion was going to catch him. He dropped to his knees and prayed, "Lord, please make this lion a Christian!" Instantly, the lion dropped to his knees. He folded his forepaws, praying, "Dear Lord, for this meal I'm about to enjoy..."

DAY 223

Today's Thought

A lot of kneeling will keep you in good standing.

Day 224

Always With You

*Surely I am with you always,
to the very end of the age.*

Matthew 28:20

Day 225

God Is a Father Like No Other

Your heavenly Father...

- always keeps His promises.
- never holds a grudge.
- is never too busy to listen.
- doesn't make mistakes.
- doesn't compare you to anyone else.
- will never leave you.
- offers love that will never fail.

DAY 226

Mercy Me

*Blessed are the merciful,
for they will be shown mercy.*

Matthew 5:7

Day 227

The Money Catch-22

To be clever enough to get all the money, one must be stupid enough to want it.

G. K. Chesterton

DAY 228

Today's Thought

It is a blessing to work for the Lord. The work is hard; the pay is low. But the retirement benefits are out of this world.

Day 229

Love Overflowing

May the Master pour on the love so it fills your lives and splashes over on everyone around you.

1 Thessalonians 3:12 MSG

DAY 230

Beyond Your Imagination...

Now to him who is able to do immeasurably more than all we ask or imagine, according to his power that is at work within us, to him be glory in the church and in Christ Jesus throughout all generations, for ever and ever! Amen.

EPHESIANS 3:20–21

Day 231

Joy in the Journey

To travel hopefully is a better thing than to arrive.

Robert Louis Stevenson

DAY 232

Good Deeds Are Great

The smallest good deed is greater than the grandest good intention.

JAPANESE PROVERB

Day 233

A Prayer for Today

Lord, show us Your way.
Lord, lead us to Your
destination. We thank You
for being our beacon of hope,
a beacon we can always
see, if we will only look.
Amen.

Day 234

The Great Eraser

*Love covers over
a multitude of sins.*

1 Peter 4:8

DAY 235

A Humble Offer

So humble yourselves under the mighty power of God, and at the right time he will lift you up in honor. Give all your worries and cares to God, for he cares about you.

1 Peter 5:6–7 NLT

DAY 236

Happiness May Appear Smaller Than It Is

Happiness always looks small while you hold it in your hands, but let it go, and you learn at once how big and precious it is.

MAKSIM GORKY

DAY 237

Like a Good Mother...

As a mother comforts her child, so will I comfort you.

ISAIAH 66:13

DAY 238

Today's Thought

Every few years, some guy says he's found Noah's ark. Why is it always Noah's ark—never Goliath's sandals, Lot's pillar-of-salt wife, or something like that?

Day 239

The Power of Prayer

The prayer of a righteous person is powerful and effective.

JAMES 5:16

Day 240

You're Gifted!

Every good and perfect gift is from above, coming down from the Father of the heavenly lights, who does not change like shifting shadows. He chose to give us birth through the word of truth, that we might be a kind of firstfruits of all he created.

James 1:17–18

DAY 241

A "Homemade" Prayer of Thanks

Dear Lord, thank You for my home. I ask that You fill it with Your Holy Spirit. Even when I don't have time to polish and dust, may it still shine with Your welcome and love, so that whoever comes in my doors senses that You are present.

ELLYN SANNA

DAY 242

Beauty Is Everywhere

Never lose an opportunity of seeing anything that is beautiful; for beauty is God's handwriting— a wayside sacrament. Welcome it in every fair face, in every fair sky, in every fair flower, and thank God for it as a cup of blessing.

RALPH WALDO EMERSON

DAY 243

If I Can...

If I can stop one
heart from breaking,
I shall not live in vain;
If I can ease one
life the aching,
Or cool one pain,
Or help one fainting robin
Unto his nest again,
I shall not live in vain.

EMILY DICKINSON

DAY 244

Never-Ending Refills

An infinite God can give all of Himself to each of His children. He does not distribute Himself that each may have a part, but to each one He gives all of Himself as fully as if there were no others.

A. W. TOZER

DAY 245

The Happy Choice

Most folks are as happy as they make up their minds to be.

ABRAHAM LINCOLN

Day 246

Not Guilty

So now there is no condemnation for those who belong to Christ Jesus.

Romans 8:1 NLT

Day 247

Four Ways God Answers Prayer

No, not yet.
No, I love you too much.
Yes, I thought you'd never ask.
Yes, and here's more.

ANNE LEWIS

DAY 248

All I Need

All I really need is love, but a little chocolate now and then doesn't hurt!

Lucy van Pelt

Day 249

Everyday Grace

Your worst days are never so bad that you are beyond the reach of God's grace. And your best days are never so good that you are beyond the need of God's grace.

Jerry Bridges

DAY 250

A World-Class Philosophy

Pray hard, work hard,
and leave the rest to God.

FLORENCE GRIFFITH JOYNER,
WORLD-CLASS SPRINTER

Day 251

For Your Inspiration...

At age forty-one, Dara Torres abandoned retirement to earn a spot on the 2008 US Olympic swim team—setting an American record in the 50-meter freestyle at the Olympic Trials. She then won three silver medals at the Beijing Games. This marked the third time Torres had come out of retirement. She plans to compete in the 2012 Olympics, at age forty-five.

Day 252

God Goes All out for You

*God, your God,
will outdo himself in
making things go well for you.*

Deuteronomy 30:8–9 msg

Day 253

Do the Right Thing

Always do right.
This will gratify some
and astonish the rest.

MARK TWAIN

DAY 254

Today's Thought

If at first you *do* succeed…
try not to look so astonished.

Day 255

Our Compassionate Lord

*The LORD longs to be gracious
to you; therefore he will rise
up to show you compassion....
Blessed are all who wait for him!*

ISAIAH 30:18

DAY 256

Heaven Heals It All

Earth hath no sorrow
that heaven cannot heal.

THOMAS MOORE

Day 257

One Matters

I am only one, but I am one. I cannot do everything, but I can do something. And that which I can do, by the grace of God, I will do.

Dwight L. Moody

DAY 258

Failure is an opportunity

Failure is the opportunity
to begin again—
more intelligently.

HENRY FORD

Day 259

The Procrastinator's Creed

I believe that if anything is worth doing, it would have been done already!

DAY 260

Your Fail-Safe

Cast your cares on the L<small>ORD</small> and He will sustain you; He will never let the righteous be shaken.

P<small>SALM</small> 55:22

Day 261

Close to the Brokenhearted

*The LORD is close to
the brokenhearted, and he
saves those whose spirits
have been crushed.*

Psalm 34:18 NCV

DAY 262

Doing Without

To be without some of the things you want is an indispensable part of happiness.

BERTRAND RUSSELL

DAY 263

Today's Thought

We don't need to keep reliving hard times. God wants to help us heal the hole in our souls. However, we can recycle those hard times in ways that help others heal. Our most painful experiences can become wise teachers.

Day 264

Like Lending to the Lord

Being kind to the poor is like lending to the Lord; he will reward you for what you have done.

Proverbs 19:17 NCV

DAY 265

Sleep Well

A quiet conscience
sleeps in thunder.

ENGLISH PROVERB

DAY 266

Did You Know?

According to nutritionist Pamela Smith, one hundred laughs a day provide a cardiovascular workout equal to about ten minutes of rowing or biking. Additionally, laughter stimulates stress release in the same way exercise does. Laughter, Smith notes, also helps fight infection by sending into the bloodstream hormones that reduce stress's immune-system-weakening power.

Day 267

A Verse to Live By

In 1922, a thirty-eight-year-old man went bankrupt in the clothing business. But he didn't give up. He pursued success, reading his favorite scripture every day. Twenty-three years later, Harry S. Truman was president. The verse that motivated him? "For I know the plans I have for you," declares the Lord, "plans to prosper you. . .to give you hope and a future" (Jeremiah 29:11).

Day 268

Good Medicine

A happy heart is good medicine.

Proverbs 17:22 AMP

Day 269

Today's Thought

Cy Young is considered by some experts to be the best baseball pitcher of all time. The annual award for the best pitcher bears his name. During his career, Young racked up an incredible 511 victories, but he also lost 315 games. Great success does not come without some failures along the way.

Day 270

Keep on Truckin'

Blessed is the man who keeps on going when times are hard.

James 1:12 NIrV

Day 271

Today's Thought

You are here for a purpose. The all-powerful Master Creator of the universe made you in His image, and He loves you intensely and personally. He has a plan for your life.

Day 272

The Cans and Cannots of Money

Money can buy you a bed, but not sleep; books, but not brains; food, but not an appetite; fitness equipment, but not fitness itself; surface beauty, but not inner beauty; a house, but not a home; medicine, but not health; amusement, but not happiness; watches and clocks, but not time.

Day 273

Mr. Know-It-All

Your heavenly Father already knows all your needs. Seek the Kingdom of God above all else, and live righteously, and he will give you everything you need. So don't worry about tomorrow.

MATTHEW 6:32–34 NLT

DAY 274

Word Countdown

Four most important words:
What is YOUR opinion?

Three most important words:
If you please.

Two most important words:
Thank you.

One most important word: *We.*

The least important word: *I.*

UNKNOWN

DAY 275

Joyous Empathy

To be able to find joy in another's joy, that is the secret of happiness.

GEORGE BERNANOS

DAY 276

Think Change Is Impossible?

Gerald R. Ford—a model turned US president

Dean Martin—a steel worker turned entertainer

Golda Meir—a schoolteacher turned prime minister

Babe Ruth—a bartender turned baseball player

DAY 277

A Work in Progress

God is not finished with us by a long shot. As I entered the prayer room today, I was reminded again that this is really about Him. He has called us to keep praying.

ANONYMOUS ENTRY ON THE
HOPE MISSIONARY CHURCH
ONLINE PRAYER ROOM

Day 278

Today's Thought

God thinks so much
of human beings that He
made His Son one of us.

DAY 279

Like the one and only

God loves each of us as if there were only one of us.

SAINT AUGUSTINE

Day 280

Homecoming

Come back to the Lord your God, because he is kind and shows mercy. He doesn't become angry quickly, and he has great love.

JOEL 2:13 NCV

Day 281

Today's Thought

When we are able to see ourselves as Jesus sees us, we obtain a sense of security and peace of mind. It gives us perspective. It gives us strength. When you understand that Jesus loves you and has your back *always*, it revolutionizes the way you interact with the people around you.

Day 282

Take Comfort

Praise be to the God and Father of our Lord Jesus Christ, the Father of compassion and the God of all comfort, who comforts us in all our troubles, so that we can comfort those in any trouble with the comfort we ourselves receive from God.

2 Corinthians 1:3–4

Day 283

Stiller's Secret

My father died at 102. Whenever I would ask what kept him going, he'd answer, "I never worry."

JERRY STILLER

Day 284

Saying "Grace"

Grace means God accepts me just as I am. He does not require or insist that I measure up to someone else's standard of performance. He loves me completely, thoroughly, and perfectly. There's nothing I can do to add or to detract from that love.

Mary Graham

DAY 285

Today's Thought

Your sweetest accomplishments—the ones you will remember with a smile and a grateful heart—will come to you as you see other people as God's creation and serve them accordingly. That's because serving is living like Jesus did. Throughout His life, He spelled success *S-E-R-V-E*.

Day 286

No More Tears

*And God shall wipe away
all tears from their eyes;
and there shall be no more death,
neither sorrow, nor crying,
neither shall there be any more pain:
for the former things are passed away.*

Revelation 21:4 kjv

Day 287

Cosby on Kids

Having a child is surely the most beautifully irrational act that two people in love can commit.

BILL COSBY

Day 288

Wearing Love

*Above all, clothe yourselves
with love, which binds everything
together in perfect harmony.
And let the peace of Christ
rule in your hearts.*

Colossians 3:14–15 nrsv

DAY 289

Signs You're Studying Too Hard

You find yourself highlighting portions of a restaurant menu.

You enter your student ID on the microwave.

Your love letters contain bullet points and outlines.

When you talk in your sleep, you recite the names of all the US presidents.

DAY 290

Think Change Is Impossible? (Part 2)

Boris Karloff—a Realtor turned horror-flick actor

Clark Gable—a lumberjack turned actor

Paul Gaugin—a stockbroker turned artist

Steve Martin—a magician turned comedian

Albert Einstein—a patent-office clerk turned physicist

Day 291

Surprised by Joy

Into all lives, in many simple, familiar, homely ways, God infuses this element of joy from the surprises of life, which unexpectedly brighten our days, and fill our eyes with light.

HENRY WADSWORTH LONGFELLOW

Day 292

Today's Thought

God has blessings with *your* name on them. He doesn't send blessings addressed to Occupant, like the junk flyers that show up in your mailbox.

Day 293

An Atheist Holiday?

An atheist complained to a friend because Christians have special holidays like Christmas and Easter, and Jews celebrate national holidays like Passover and Yom Kippur. "We atheists," he said, "have no recognized national holiday. It is unfair discrimination." To which his friend replied, "Why don't you celebrate April 1st?"

DAY 294

Just Rewards

The highest reward for your work is not what you get for it, but what you become by it.

JOHN C. MAXWELL

DAY 295

For God So Loved...

*For God so loved the world,
that he gave his only begotten Son,
that whosoever believeth
in him should not perish,
but have everlasting life.*

JOHN 3:16 KJV

Day 296

What a Friend We Have in Jesus

What a friend we have in Jesus,
All our sins and griefs to bear!
What a privilege to carry
Everything to God in prayer!
O what peace we often forfeit,
O what needless pain we bear,
All because we do not carry
Everything to God in prayer.

Joseph M. Scriven

DAY 297

Grace Is Enough

The grace of God is sufficient
for all our needs, for every
problem, and for every difficulty,
for every broken heart,
and for every human sorrow.

PETER MARSHALL

Day 298

What's in a Name?

A good name is to be chosen rather than great riches, loving favor rather than silver and gold.

Proverbs 22:1 NKJV

Day 299

He Who Holds Tomorrow

Do not look forward to
what may happen tomorrow;
the same everlasting Father who
cares for you today will take care
of you tomorrow and every day.
Either He will shield you from suffering,
or He will give you unfailing strength
to bear it. Be at peace then,
and put aside all anxious
thoughts and imaginations.

Saint Francis de Sales

Day 300

Your Heavenly Citizenship

Our citizenship is in heaven. And we eagerly await a Savior from there.

PHILIPPIANS 3:20

Day 301

Poetic Justice

One of the greatest American poets was a failure for some twenty years! He was thirty-nine before he ever sold a volume of poetry. Today, he is considered one of the finest writers ever. He's been published in more than twenty languages. He won the Pulitzer Prize for poetry four times! Congress named him an American Poet Laureate. He is Robert Frost.

DAY 302

On Love and Baseball...

Love is the most important thing in the world, but baseball is pretty good, too.

YOGI BERRA

DAY 303

Today's Thought

Don't worry too much about being punctual. Usually, there's no one there to appreciate it.

Day 304

The City of God

*As we have heard,
so we have seen in the city
of the Lord Almighty, in the city
of our God: God makes
her secure forever.*

Psalm 48:8

DAY 305

One Size Fits All

No problem is so big that it won't fit in God's hands.

SUZANNE BERRY

Day 306

Today's Thought

Even if you've fished for three hours and gotten nothing but a sunburn and a backache…you're still better off than the worm!

Day 307

One Solitary Light

All the darkness in the world cannot extinguish the light of a single candle.

SAINT FRANCIS

DAY 308

Today's Thought

You look just as good as any model...when you yawn!

Day 309

on the Battle of the Sexes...

No one will ever win the battle of the sexes. There's too much fraternizing with the enemy.

HENRY KISSINGER

Day 310

The Essence of Art

Creativity is allowing
yourself to make mistakes.
Art is knowing which
ones to keep.

SCOTT ADAMS

Day 311

Why Angels Can Fly

Angels can fly because they take themselves lightly.

G. K. Chesterton

DAY 312

Today's Thought

The harder the wind blows,
the higher the kite will fly.

Day 313

What Can't God Do?

With God nothing shall be impossible.

Luke 1:37 KJV

DAY 314

Happiness Is...

Happiness is getting a brown gravy stain on a brown dress.

TOTIE FIELDS

DAY 315

LOL!

If you're going to laugh,
go ahead and laugh out loud.

CYNTHIA LEWIS

DAY 316

It's What's Inside That Counts

The kingdom of God is within you.

Luke 17:21 NKJV

Day 317

Attitude Counts!

Whoever said math is a drag never tried counting jelly beans.

Bryce Hafer

DAY 318

Did You Know?

Babe Ruth struck out 1,330 times en route to his 714 home runs.

Day 319

Go With a Winner

The Lord will march out like a champion, like a warrior he will stir up his zeal; with a shout he will raise the battle cry and will triumph over his enemies.

Isaiah 42:13

Day 320

Darkness into Light

*You, Lord, are my lamp;
the Lord turns my
darkness into light.*

2 Samuel 22:29

DAY 321

The Size of Grace

God's grace is too big, too great to understand fully. So we must take the moments of His grace throughout the day with us; the music of the songbird in the morning, the kindness shown in the afternoon, and the restful sleep at night.

UNKNOWN

Day 322

Pressing Forward

*Forgetting what is behind and
straining toward what is ahead,
I press on toward the goal to win the
prize for which God has called me
heavenward in Christ Jesus.*

Philippians 3:13–14

Day 323

The Power of a Kiss

A little kiss can make a big difference.

CYNTHIA LEWIS

Day 324

Mind over Matter

Age is an issue of mind over matter. If you don't mind, it doesn't matter.

Mark Twain

Day 325

Standing Firm

[God] gives us the victory through our Lord Jesus Christ. Therefore, my dear brothers and sisters, stand firm. Let nothing move you.

1 Corinthians 15:57–58

Day 326

Safe and Secure

God, whose very own you are,
will lead you safely through all things.
And when you cannot stand it,
God will carry you in His arms.

SAINT FRANCIS DE SALES

Day 327

Every Little Thing

Whatever we do in God's name, in His spirit, always matters. God can do small, simple things that make people's lives a little bit better.

Toby Mac

DAY 328

God's Tools

Troubles are often the tools by which God fashions us for better things.

HENRY WARD BEECHER

DAY 329

Start with a Smile

Start every day off with a smile and get it over with.

W. C. FIELDS

Day 330

Older and Wiser

Dr. George Lawson, a gerontologist, notes, "Your mind is still young at fifty—your brain doesn't reach its zenith until ten years after that. And from sixty on, mental efficiency declines very slowly to the age of eighty. At eighty, you can be just as productive mentally as you were at thirty—and you should know a lot more."

Day 331

Sing for Joy!

Sing a new song to the Lord, for he has done wonderful deeds. His right hand has won a mighty victory; his holy arm has shown his saving power!

Psalm 98:1 NLT

DAY 332

A Heavenly Shock Absorber

God doesn't always smooth the path, but sometimes He puts springs in the wagon.

MARSHALL LUCAS

Day 333

To Give Is to Receive

Those who bring happiness to the lives of others cannot keep it from themselves.

Sir James Barrie

DAY 334

Fear = Happiness?

How joyful are those who fear the Lord.... They are confident and fearless and can face their foes triumphantly.

Psalm 112:1, 8 NLT

Day 335

Gaining Years, Gaining Memories

The great thing about getting older is that you don't lose all the other ages you've been.

MADELEINE L'ENGLE

Day 336

More Than Conquerors

In all these things we are more than conquerors through him who loved us.

ROMANS 8:37

DAY 337

Life on the Fast Track

If everything is under control,
you are going too slow.

MARIO ANDRETTI,
LEGENDARY RACE-CAR DRIVER

DAY 338

Go Big

Go confidently in the
direction of your dreams.
Live the life you have imagined.

HENRY DAVID THOREAU

Day 339

With You All the Way

The LORD will guide you always; he will satisfy your needs.

ISAIAH 58:11

Day 340

Comfort for the Sad

*God blesses those who mourn,
for they will be comforted.*

Matthew 5:4 nlt

Day 341

When It Rains...

When it rains on your parade,
look up rather than down.
Without the rain,
there would be no rainbow.

G. K. CHESTERTON

Day 342

Getting and Giving the Best

Give the world the best
you have and the best will
come back to you.

MADELINE BRIDGES

Day 343

Our 24-7 Lord

God is faithful still,
and hears prayers still.

GEORGE MUELLER

Day 344

A Prayer of Perspective

Dear Loving God,
Help me to remember,
when I start to lose hope,
that all the darkness in
the world is just a speck
in Your light, a light that
fills the whole universe.
Amen.

Day 345

The Art of Life

Make each day your masterpiece.

Coach John Wooden

Day 346

The Joy of Friendship

Life's truest happiness is found in the friendships we make along the way.

R. BENNETT

Day 347

Rock Solid

"Though the mountains be shaken and the hills be removed, yet my unfailing love for you will not be shaken nor my covenant of peace be removed," says the LORD, who has compassion on you.

Isaiah 54:10

Day 348

Our Compassionate Lord

The Lord longs to be gracious to you; therefore he will rise up to show you compassion.... Blessed are all who wait for him!

Isaiah 30:18

Day 349

Enjoy Those Kids!

We find a delight in the beauty and happiness of children that makes the heart too big for the body.

Ralph Waldo Emerson

Day 350

Blessings Abounding

*The faithful will
abound with blessings.*

Proverbs 28:20 nrsv

Day 351

God Is Pure Love

God loves you simply because he has chosen to do so. He loves you when you don't feel lovely. He loves you when no one else loves you. God will love you always. No matter what.

MAX LUCADO

Day 352

He Will Lead You

With all your heart you must trust the LORD and not your own judgment. Always let him lead you, and he will clear the road for you to follow.

PROVERBS 3:5–6 CEV

Day 353

You Are a Chosen One!

He chose us in Him before the foundation of the world... according to the good pleasure of His will, to the praise of the glory of His grace, by which He made us accepted in the Beloved.

Ephesians 1:4–6 NKJV

Day 354

Safe and Secure

God is our refuge and strength.

Psalm 46:1 KJV

Day 355

Today's Thought

The road ahead of you might be completely unfamiliar and intimidating. You might not know where the road will ultimately lead. But if you travel it hand in hand with God, your journey and your destination will be truly rewarding.

DAY 356

God's Work of Art

*We are God's handiwork,
created in Christ Jesus
to do good works,
which God prepared in
advance for us to do.*

EPHESIANS 2:10

DAY 357

Success Isn't Everything

About the only problem with success is that it does not teach you how to deal with failure.

TOMMY LASORDA,
LEGENDARY BASEBALL MANAGER

DAY 358

You're Gifted!

We are all gifted.
That is our inheritance.

ETHEL WATERS

Day 359

Never Give Up!

It's always too soon to quit.

RAY CROC,
FOUNDER OF MCDONALD'S

Day 360

To Be Remembered...

If you want to be remembered after you're dead, write something worth reading or do something worth writing about.

BENJAMIN FRANKLIN

Day 361

A Prayer of Thanks

Dear Loving Creator,
Thank You for creating me,
a unique person in the
entire world and loving me
personally. May I sense Your
love and acceptance every day.
Yes, I am a work in progress—
that's for sure. But I am
Your work in progress.
Amen.

Day 362

Endless Echoes of Kindness

Kind words can be short and easy to speak, but their echoes are truly endless.

MOTHER TERESA

Day 363

A Blessed Home

*He blesses the home
of the righteous.*

Proverbs 3:33

Day 364

No Matter What...

When you're in over your head, I'll be there with you. When you're in rough waters, you will not go down. When you're between a rock and a hard place, it won't be a dead end—because I am God, your personal God.

Isaiah 43:2–3 msg

DAY 365

A Happy Ending

I've read the last page of the Bible. It's all going to turn out all right.

BILLY GRAHAM

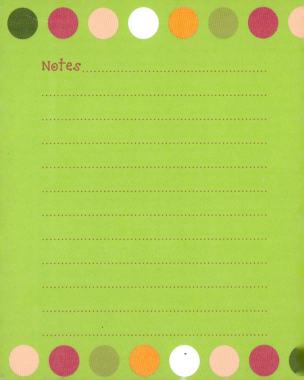

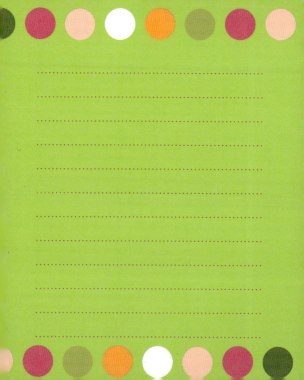

Notes

Notes

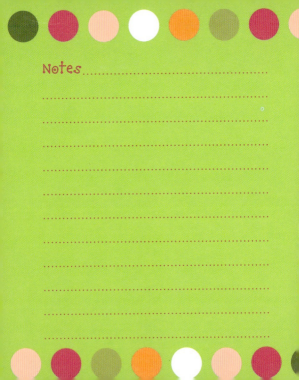

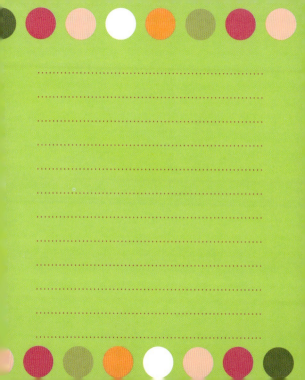

Notes

Notes

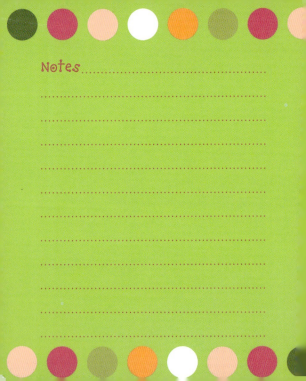